W9-DEA-428

CUSTOMER FOCUS

A Strategy for Success

CUSTOMER FOCUS
A Strategy for Success

ROGER G. LANGEVIN

CRISP PUBLICATIONS

Editor-in-Chief: *William F. Christopher*

Project Editor: *Kathleen Barcos*

Editor: *Amy Marks*

Cover Design: *Kathleen Barcos*

Cover Production: *Russell Leong Design*

Book Design & Production: *London Road Design*

Printer: *Bawden Printing*

Library of Congress Card Catalog Number 98-72276

ISBN 1-56052-485-5

To Catherine, for her expertise,
Karen, for her professionalism,
Linda, for her dependability,
and, of course, to
Carolyn, for her thoughtfulness.

CONTENTS

INTRODUCTION

In today's rapidly changing and extremely competitive environment, customers demand greater value and higher satisfaction levels. As a strategic concept, customer-driven quality and service—directed toward customer retention and market share growth—can effectively provide competitive advantage. This advantage can be achieved only when processes are systematically aligned with customer expectations and companywide business goals and when meaningful performance measures are used to drive improvement actions. Customer focus is one of the most critical factors essential for success in today's business marketplace.

This book provides a succinct road map for enhancing customer satisfaction and outlines steps to improve operational performance throughout the organization.

Chapter 1 features the significance of *customer focus*. The chapter highlights the Malcolm Baldrige National Quality Award Criteria for Performance Excellence with emphasis on customer and market knowledge, customer satisfaction results and relationship enhancement. Key excellence examples from selected Baldrige winners are presented.

Chapter 2 introduces a series of *quality system standards*, including the International Organization for Standardization (ISO) series, and requirements for the automotive and aerospace industries.

Chapter 3 treats the various aspects of *market research* as a powerful tool to drive improvement actions throughout the organization. Appropriate methodologies are compared, and guidance on research deployment and meaningful analysis is presented.

Chapter 4 addresses the *process management* issues critical for achieving performance excellence, emphasizing the need for heightened quality and service awareness. The total quality management concept is summarized. Process analysis and quality planning approaches are outlined.

Chapter 5 summarizes the *quality improvement process.* Steps for achieving self-sufficiency and performance excellence are outlined with a focus on problem solving. A variety of quality improvement tools are introduced.

Chapter 6 stresses the importance of meaningful *performance measurement*—including the need for linkage to, and alignment with, the company's business plans and strategies.

In several chapters, how-to guidance is presented in the spirit of the Chinese proverb:

> *Give a man a fish and*
> *you feed him for a day.*
> *Teach a man to fish and*
> *you feed him for a lifetime.*

I.

CUSTOMER FOCUS

*The United States is the most competitive nation
in the world. Quality is a key to retaining that title.
The Malcolm Baldrige National Quality Award is
helping U.S. companies satisfy customers and improve
overall company performance and capabilities.*

William J. Clinton

More than ever before, customers are demanding
greater value of delivered products and services
and expecting higher levels of satisfaction. As
we move into the twenty-first century, even greater competition and tougher challenges will be present in the marketplace. Customer-driven quality and service will be critical
for future success. Only through customer focus will organizations be able to gain essential competitive advantage.

The Malcolm Baldrige National Quality Award
Criteria—when understood and deployed in an organization—can be a very effective tool, or road map, for continuous quality improvement and is an excellent framework
for achieving market success and competitive advantage.
Named after the former United States Secretary of Com-
merce, The Malcolm Baldrige National Quality Improvement Act, Public Law 100-107, signed by President Reagan

in 1987, established the annual U.S. National Quality Award. The purposes of the Award are to promote quality awareness, to recognize quality achievement of U.S. companies, and to publicize successful strategies. The Award criteria are designed to help companies enhance their competitiveness through delivery of ever-improving value to customers, resulting in marketplace success.

The Baldrige Framework

The Malcolm Baldrige National Quality Award Criteria are recognized worldwide as a powerful vehicle for strengthening and integrating business performance and competitiveness. The criteria have been strengthened and refined each year since the initial applications were submitted in 1988. More than 60 state or regional quality award programs in 36 states have been established, most of them modeled on the Baldrige framework. Throughout the United States, many companies and organizations have adopted the Baldrige Criteria as their management system model for self-assessment and business improvement. Many other countries have also established national awards similar to the Baldrige Criteria. The European Quality Award has been adopted widely in Europe as a model for self-appraisal.

As adopted by Congress, the legislation states: ". . .strategic planning for quality and quality improvement programs, through a commitment to excellence in manufacturing and services, are becoming more and more essential to the well-being of our Nation's economy and our ability to compete effectively in the global marketplace." Further, the legislation emphasizes that ". . . in order to be successful, quality improvement programs must be management-led and customer-oriented, and this may require fundamental changes in the way companies and agencies do business." The Award promotes an understanding of the requirements for performance excellence and competitiveness improvement and encourages the sharing of information on successful performance strategies. Manufacturing companies, service companies and small businesses (with not more than 500 full-time employees) are eligible to apply. Pilot programs are currently under way to expand the fields of eligibility to the health-care field and the education sector.

Award Criteria

The Award Criteria for Performance Excellence are built upon a set of *core values and concepts* that serve as the foundation for integrating key business requirements within a results-oriented framework:

- Customer-driven Quality

- Leadership

- Continuous Improvement and Learning

- Employee Participation and Development

- Fast Response

- Design Quality and Prevention

- Long-range View of the Future

- Management by Fact
- Partnership Development
- Company Responsibility and Citizenship
- Results Focus

The core values and concepts are embodied in seven categories, within which are twenty *evaluation items* with specific areas to address, each typically focusing on a major requirement:

1. Leadership
   - Leadership System
   - Company Responsibility and Citizenship

2. Strategic Planning
   - Strategy Development Process
   - Company Strategy

3. Customer and Market Focus
   - Customer and Market Knowledge
   - Customer Satisfaction and Relationship Enhancement

4. Information and Analysis
   - Selection and Use of Information and Data
   - Selection and Use of Comparative Information and Data
   - Analysis and Review of Company Performance

5. Human Resource Development and Management

- Work Systems
- Employee Education, Training and Development
- Employee Well-being and Satisfaction

6. Process Management
   - Management of Product and Service Processes
   - Management of Support Processes
   - Management of Supplier and Partnering Processes

7. Business Results
   - Customer Satisfaction Results
   - Financial and Market Results
   - Human Resource Results
   - Supplier and Partner Results
   - Company-specific Results

The Baldrige Award Criteria and framework provide a customer- and market-focused perspective by connecting and integrating three basic elements: strategy and action plans, systems, and information and analysis (see Figure 1).

- *Strategy and action plans* guide overall resource decisions and drive the alignment of measures for all work units to ensure customer satisfaction and market success.

- *Systems* define the organization, its operations and its results (a composite of customer, financial and nonfinancial performance).

- *Information and analysis* are critical to the effective management of the company and to a fact-based system for improving company performance and competitiveness.

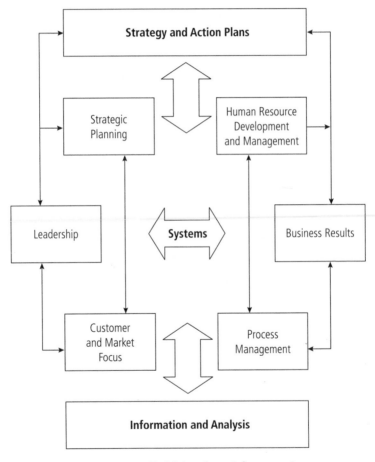

Figure 1.   Baldrige Award framework

Customer and Market Focus

Within the Baldrige Criteria, the Customer and Market Focus category examines how the company determines the requirements and expectations of its customers and markets. The category also examines how the company enhances customer relationships and determines customer satisfaction.

The first evaluation item in this category, Customer and Market Knowledge, provides criteria for how the company determines longer-term requirements, expectations and preferences of target and potential customers and markets. This item explores how the company learns from its current and potential customers and markets to develop and support the company's overall business needs and opportunities, including:

- How customer groups and market segments are determined or selected, including the consideration of competitors' customers and other potential customers and markets—and how the approaches to listening and learning vary for different customer groups

- How key product and service features and their relative importance and value to customers are determined and projected—and how such key information, including customer retention and complaint information, is used in this determination

- How the company's approach to listening to, and learning from, customers and markets is evaluated, improved and kept current with changing business needs

The second evaluation item, Customer Satisfaction and Relationship Enhancement, provides criteria on how the company determines and enhances the satisfaction of its customers to strengthen relationships, improve current offerings and support customer- and market-related planning. This item explores how the company provides access and information to its customers and how customer satisfaction is determined:

- Accessibility and Complaint Management: how the company determines customer contact requirements, deploys the requirements to employees and evaluates and improves customer contact performance; and how the company's complaint management process is evaluated to ensure that complaints are resolved effectively and promptly, and that all complaints are aggregated and analyzed for use throughout the company

- Customer Satisfaction Determination: how the company follows up with customers on products, services and recent transactions to receive prompt and actionable feedback; how other processes and measurements of customer satisfaction are used to capture actionable information that addresses customers' future business; and how the company obtains objective and reliable information on customer satisfaction relative to its competitors

In the Business Results category, the company's business results, performance and improvement are examined in key business areas—customer satisfaction, financial marketplace performance, human resources, supplier and partner performance and company-specific operational performance–as well as performance levels relative to competitors. Customer satisfaction measurements might include both a numerical rating scale and descriptors for each unit in the scale. The effective, or actionable, measurement of customer satisfaction provides reliable information about how customers rate specific product and service features and the relationship between these ratings and the customer's likely future actions.

The Customer Satisfaction Results item addresses the current levels and trends in key measures and indicators of customer satisfaction and dissatisfaction, including satisfaction relative to competitors. Such measures and indicators may include information on customer-perceived value. Objective information and data may come from customers and independent organizations.

The underlying premise for customer-driven quality is that quality is judged by customers–and must take into account all product and service features that contribute value to customers and lead to customer satisfaction, preference and retention. It means much more than reducing the number of defects and errors, merely meeting specifications or lowering the number of complaints. Nevertheless, eliminating the causes of dissatisfaction contributes to the customer's view of quality and is crucial to building customer relationships and to shaping customer perception. Thus, customer-driven quality is a strategic concept directed toward customer retention, market share gain and growth. It demands constant sensitivity to changing and emerging customer and market requirements and to the factors that drive customer satisfaction and retention.

Examples of Excellence

In any one year, no more than two companies can win the National Quality Award in each of the three eligibility categories, i.e., manufacturing companies, service companies and small businesses. In the Award's first ten years, only 32 companies won the coveted Award—or an average of three per year—just about half of the number of awards that could have been given (see Figure 2).

Each of the winners has demonstrated exemplary performance when judged against the stringent criteria for performance excellence. Upon applying for, and winning, the Award, companies are expected to share information on successful performance strategies, and the benefits derived from using those strategies, with other organizations in the United States. Some illustrations of Baldrige Award winners exemplifying excellent customer focus follow:

- **AT&T Network Systems Group, Transmission Systems Business Unit (TSBU):** the nation's largest maker of transmission equipment for telecommunications networks. TSBU uses feedback from customer report cards to implement process improvements, offers a risk-free trial of new products, and rewards employees who exceed customer expectations. TSBU's goal is to promptly resolve all customer

1997: Merrill Lynch Credit Corporation
3M Dental Products Division
Solectron Corporation
Xerox Business Services

1996: ADAC Laboratories
Custom Research, Inc.
Dana Commercial Credit Corporation
Trident Precision Manufacturing, Inc.

1995: Armstrong World Industries, Inc.—Building Products Operations
Corning, Inc.—Telecommunications/Products Division

1994: AT&T Consumer Communications Services
GTE Directories Corporations
Wainwright Industries, Inc.

1993: Ames Rubber Company
Eastman Chemical Company

1992: AT&T Network Systems Group—Transmission Systems Business Unit
AT&T Universal Card Services
Granite Rock Company
Texas Instruments, Inc.—Defense Systems & Electronics Group
The Ritz-Carlton Hotel Company

1991: Marlow Industries, Inc.
Solectron Corporation
Zytec Corporation

1990: Cadillac Motor Car Company
Federal Express Corporation
IBM Rochester
Wallace Co., Inc.

1989: Milliken & Company
Xerox Corporation—Business Products and Systems

1988: Globe Metallurgical, Inc.
Motorola, Inc.
Westinghouse Electric Corporation—Commercial Nuclear Fuel Division

Figure 2. Malcolm Baldrige National Quality Award winners

issues, and 98% of inquiries are resolved by technical support representatives on initial contact.

- **AT&T Universal Card Services (UCS):** markets and provides custom services for the AT&T Universal Card. UCS uses monthly customer surveys, telephone interviews, frequent customer contacts and call monitoring by associates and senior executives to determine customer satisfaction. Fundamental to the aim of "delighting customers," and in recognition of the need to listen to customers, UCS established four key "listening posts"—customer expectation and needs research, performance research, direct customer feedback and process management. Information is obtained through eleven monthly surveys tracking overall satisfaction and service quality and is compiled in eight databases of customer-related information. A cross-functional group of employees, called the Customer Listening Post Team, aggregates and acts upon the sources of data when complex issues are identified. UCS offers an explicit commitment to its customers—the Service Quality Warranty—promising "A Trusted Partner, Entitlement to Error-free Service, Availability When You Need Us, Quick Action to Protect Your Interests, and More Than Just Plastic."

- **Corning Telecommunications Products Division (TPD):** the world's largest manufacturer of optical fibers. TPD has developed a strategy-driven, customer-focused system that integrates quality into all parts of the business and has customer satisfaction as a key strategic initiative. TPD's integrated approach to interacting with existing and prospective customers includes its Customer Response System for gathering customer inputs, establishing priorities and initiating action plans to increase levels of customer satisfaction. Information is collected in a variety of ways—through surveys, customer report cards, competitive comparisons, focus groups and other means of assessing customer satisfaction and perceptions of quality—and is organized in a customer database that is accessible to all employees.

- **Custom Research, Inc. (CRI):** a national marketing research firm. CRI has adopted a "customer-as-partner" approach, and the goal of its customer-focused teams is to "surprise and delight" their clients. At the end of each project, customers are surveyed to solicit an overall satisfaction rating based on their overall expectations. End-of-project evaluations are also conducted for CRI support teams and suppliers. Five key business drivers are the points of CRI's star-shaped icon: people, processes, requirements, relationships and results.

- **Eastman Chemical Company:** supplies chemicals, fibers and plastics. Under the umbrella of Eastman's companywide Making Eastman the Preferred Supplier (MEPS) process, over 250 teams with 700 participants have been formed, and more than 100 teams have completed projects with a primary focus on improving customer satisfaction. The MEPS process begins with listening to the "voice of the customer" to determine customer needs. Upon completion of each project, the team presents the improvements to customers.

- **Granite Rock Company:** producer of construction materials. At Granite Rock, ultimate customer satisfaction is assured through a system in which customers can choose not to pay for a product or service that doesn't meet their expectations. This unique "short-pay" system gives customers a simple procedure for resolving deficiencies while at the same time provides timely feedback.

- **IBM Rochester:** provider of the AS/400 family of computers and advanced direct-access storage products. IBM's focus on customer relationships has been achieved through four market-driven principles: "make the customer the final arbiter, understand our markets, commit to leadership in the markets we choose to serve, and execute with excellence across the enterprise." IBM's approach to these principles has been described in five initiatives: "define the needs of the market, eliminate defects, reduce the total cycle time, increase employee participation, and measure progress." Rochester stands as the model in IBM's drive to achieve total customer satisfaction. Senior executives were named as owners of the initiatives, and specific processes to accomplish them were deployed.

- **The Ritz-Carlton Hotel Company:** a management company that develops and operates luxury hotels. Each Ritz-Carlton employee participates in a 21-day orientation including 100 hours of service and quality training. Employees are supported by a system detailing guests' preferences and have a $2,000 spending authority—with which they are empowered to do whatever it takes to provide "instant pacification." The company's Gold Standard, which has been established for each employee position, includes a credo, motto, three steps of service, and twenty Ritz-Carlton Basics—standards each employee is expected to understand and adhere to.

- **Texas Instruments, Inc., Defense Systems and Electronics Group:** maker of precision-guided weapons and other advanced defense technology. Texas Instrument's (TI's) fundamental objective of Customer Satisfaction through Total Quality is achieved through three elements (customer focus, continuous improvement and people involvement) and five thrusts (customer satisfaction, stretch goals, benchmarking, teamwork and empowerment, and integrated total quality), and is measured by four performance metrics (meeting customer commitments, quality, cycle time and training hours per person). In a survey of 2,000 customers, the company ranked number one in every attribute. TI provides special training in active listening and responsiveness and responds to all complaints in one day with complete resolution within a week.

- **Trident Precision Manufacturing, Inc.**: manufactures precision sheet-metal components, electro-mechanical assemblies and custom products for the office equipment, medical-supply, computer and defense industries. Trident has established "quality as its basic business plan" to accomplish each of its five key business drivers, all of which contribute to achieving the company's overarching aim of total customer satisfaction. Senior executives meet twice a year with representatives of each customer for in-depth discussions about Trident's performance.

Copies of the complete Malcolm Baldrige National Quality Award Criteria and other material (including a list of the winners and each of their company contacts) can be obtained free of charge from Malcolm Baldrige National Quality Award, National Institute of Standards and Technology, Route 270 and Quince Orchard Road, Administration Building, Gaithersburg, Maryland, 20899-0001.

II.

QUALITY SYSTEMS

Practice does not make perfect.
Only perfect practice makes perfect.

Vince Lombardi

Quality improvement is one of the most important corporate and international business strategies today. With the expansion of domestic and international competition, a key determinant for success in the global marketplace is higher product quality and better service levels. This focus on quality has been demonstrated by the growing emphasis on compliance with quality standards.

A *quality system* can be defined as the "organization, policy, responsibilities, procedures, processes, and resources for implementing quality management." Quality system standards have been in existence for many years. For example, during the 1950s compliance with quality system standards and specifications was mandatory in order for companies to qualify for Department of Defense contracts. During the era of the space program in the 1960s, NASA mandated compliance with its space program quality system requirements; NATO adopted a series of quality system standards; and the Nuclear Regulatory Commission required compliance with its federal regulations. More recently, the International Organization for Standardization (ISO) 9000 series of standards have been universally recognized and are being adopted by many organizations worldwide.

International Standards

The ISO was founded in 1946 to promote the development of international standards and related activities, including conformity assessments, to facilitate the exchange of goods and services worldwide. In 1987, the ISO published a series of five international standards (ISO 9000, 9001, 9002, 9003 and 9004) that provide guidance on appropriate quality management systems. The ISO 9000 Standard Series has been adopted in the United States as the American National Standards Institute (ANSI)/American Society for Quality (ASQ) Q 9000 Series. In Europe, the series has been released as the European Norm (EN) 2900 Series; and in the United Kingdom, as standard BS5750. The European Community has been a driving force behind the acceptance of ISO 9000 standards and third-party certification.

There are three primary ANSI/ISO/ASQ contractual quality standards:

- Q9001: Quality Systems–Model for Quality Assurance in Design, Development, Production, Installation and Servicing

- Q9002: Quality Systems–Model for Quality Assurance in Production, Installation and Servicing

- Q9003: Quality Systems–Model for Quality Assurance in Final Inspection and Test

Of the three standards, Q9001 prescribes the most comprehensive quality system. Q9002 does not include requirements for design control, and Q9003 is generally used where conformance to specified requirements is to be assured by the supplier solely at final inspection and test.

Additional sets of standards that provide guidance on the selection, use and implementation of ISO quality systems are listed in the Appendix.

The objectives of an ISO 9000 quality system are to achieve and sustain the quality of a product or service in order to continually meet the purchaser's stated or implied needs, to provide confidence to management that the intended quality is being achieved and sustained, and to provide confidence to the purchaser that the intended quality is being, or will be, achieved in the product delivered or the service provided.

The most comprehensive standard (Q9001) contains 20 specific quality system requirements to which organizations are expected to conform:

- Management responsibility

- Quality system

- Contract review

- Design control

- Document and data control
- Purchasing
- Control of customer-supplied product
- Product identification and traceability
- Process control
- Inspection and testing
- Control of inspection, measuring and test equipment
- Inspection and test status
- Control of nonconforming product
- Corrective and preventive action
- Handling, storage, packaging, preservation and delivery
- Control of quality records
- Internal quality audits
- Training
- Servicing
- Statistical techniques

Companies complying with ISO standards must demonstrate evidence that these quality systems are effectively in place—that procedures and work instructions are consistently implemented and comply with these systems—and that the systems are documented adequately.

The typical documentation structure consists of four levels:

- Level 1. Quality Manual: describes the organization's philosophy, policy and an overview of the quality system, including the general approach and overall responsibility for implementation

- Level 2. Procedures: defines the principles, strategies and activities of the functional units (i.e., what, when, where and who) that implement the quality system

- Level 3. Work Instructions: provides detailed descriptions of how specific job practices are performed

- Level 4. Other Documentation: includes records and evidence that demonstrate the quality system is working and/or that it complies with requirements

Automotive Industry Standards

For many years, each of the Big Three automobile makers had imposed their own quality system requirements on their suppliers. Chrysler Corporation had its Supplier Quality Assurance Manual, Ford Motor Company used its Q-101, Quality System Standard, and General Motors Corporation imposed its Targets for Excellence criteria. This arrangement made for unnecessary complexity and extreme redundancy, causing hardships on suppliers who had to comply with multiple sets of requirements.

Chrysler, Ford and General Motors recently agreed to harmonize their fundamental quality system requirements, manuals and assessment tools. QS-9000, Quality

System Requirements, was released with the goal of developing fundamental quality systems that provide for continuous improvement. The three automobile makers were committed to working with suppliers to ensure customer satisfaction—from conforming to quality requirements, to preventing defects, to reducing variation and waste in their supply chains—for the benefit of the final customer, the supply base and themselves. Suppliers who comply with the QS-9000 standard have to establish, document and implement effective quality systems in accordance with the timing requirements established by their customers. The requirements of QS-9000 are to be incorporated in the supplier's quality system and described in the supplier's quality manual.

QS-9000 consists of three sections: (I) ISO 9000-based requirements, (II) sector-specific requirements, and (III) customer-specific requirements. Additional customer reference manuals and provisions are also cited and imposed for specific requirements, including: Advanced Product Quality Planning and Control Plans, Failure Mode and Effects Analysis, Measurement Systems Analysis and Fundamental Statistical Process Control (SPC).

QS-9000 and the ISO 9000 series differ in some significant ways. QS-9000 is more prescriptive, often stating how certain things must be done. Companies complying with QS-9000 must be able to demonstrate that their quality systems are indeed effective by keeping records of gains accomplished. Companies must also manage their supplier base, monitor on-time delivery performance and track premium or excessive freight charges. Under QS-9000, suppliers must also maintain an inventory management system and a preventive maintenance plan as well as have a documented process for determining customer satisfaction with provisions for a continuous improvement system.

Copies of the QS-9000 and other manuals may be obtained from AIAG, Automotive Industry Action Group, 26200 Lahser Road, Suite 200, Southfield, Michigan, 48034.

Aerospace Industry Standards

For many years, aerospace and defense contractors were required to comply with specifications, such as MIL-Q-9858 for their quality system and MIL-I-45208 for their inspection system (both of which were canceled recently). In the industry's vision of the future, suppliers will be evaluated on the basis of data-driven measurements such as quality, delivery, responsiveness and costs. Moving toward creating a single quality system capable of meeting each customer's requirements, the Department of Defense has redefined the basic quality system standard for aerospace industry manufacturers—to "assure customer satisfaction . . . and . . . produce world-class quality products at the lowest possible cost." This initiative will standardize supplier quality system requirements by supple- menting ISO 9000 with unique aerospace-industry requirements. Other standards are being developed to prescribe industry requirements, such as requirements for the performance and documentation of first-article inspections.

The Society of Automotive Engineers–the world's largest, nongovernment producer of aerospace standards–has submitted AS9000, Aerospace Basic Quality System Standard, for recognition as an American National Standard. AS9000 reflects the provisions of ISO 9001 with specific additions and clarifications, such as the customer's right of entry to verify purchased product, delegation of supplier verification to subcontractors, requirements for the flow down of quality system requirements to subcontractors and additional controls for nonconforming product and material review. Some aerospace manufacturers have adopted the standard for their quality systems, but the extent to which these requirements will be deployed industrywide has yet to be determined.

Questions regarding the Aerospace Basic Quality System Standard (AS9000), and its appended checklist, can be addressed to the Society of Automotive Engineers, Inc., 400 Commonwealth Drive, Warrendale, Pennsylvania, 15096-0001.

III.

MARKET RESEARCH

*When used to drive improvement actions
throughout the organization, appropriately designed
and well-executed research can strengthen internal
performance and raise customer satisfaction levels.*

Karen Lynch

O ne of the necessary components of customer-driven quality is an accurate and objective understanding of customers and the many factors influencing their opinions and their perceptions. Decision makers at all levels within an organization need to listen to, and learn from, their customers in order to fully comprehend their requirements and expectations. Once these expectations are understood, an organization can measure how well it is meeting them.

Market research is an excellent tool to obtain information and further understand customers' attitudes and behavior. When implemented effectively, market research can broaden an organization's depth of understanding of its customers, provide insight into customer requirements and satisfaction levels and provide actionable data that can be used to make better decisions and thus improve business performance.

Webster's New World™ Dictionary of Media and Communications defines *market research* as "the study of the demands or desires of consumers (or other publics) in relation to actual or potential products and services." Through research, a company can determine what both its internal and external customers want and need. It does this by asking questions and listening to—and learning from—the answers.

While listening and learning enhance an organization's understanding of its customers, appropriate action must be taken to ensure customer satisfaction. Only careful planning and the systematic collection, analysis and interpretation of research data can provide insightful and actionable information. Effective research projects typically entail the following critical steps:

- Defining the objectives

- Selecting the methodology

- Performing the research

- Using the findings

Defining the Objectives

The first step for any research initiative is to fully explore objectives and critical business considerations. Strategic business goals should be recognized, and research objectives should be clearly understood. Examples of such objectives might be to:

- Investigate the emotional and psychological reasons, motivators, catalysts or triggers for purchasing specific products

- Understand the consumers' decision-making process with regard to the purchase of certain services

- Determine stakeholder preferences

- Ascertain customers' service quality expectations

- Identify areas where performance is deficient, satisfactory or higher than expected

- Recognize any gaps between perceived and expected levels of service

- Understand perceptions of an organization, particularly as compared to competitors

In establishing the research objectives, preliminary questions should be asked, such as:

- What does the organization want to find out, learn and/or gain insight into?

- What does the organization plan to do after the research is completed?

- How will the information be used?

- What might change as a result of the research?

Once these and similar questions are answered, the proper methodology can be selected.

Selecting the Methodology

Several research methodologies are available. Not only do the objectives have to be fully understood, but many other considerations need to be taken into account. First, the organization must determine the type of data it is looking for and which type would be most helpful. For the most part, research data falls into two general categories: *primary data* and *secondary data.*

Primary data are data collected by the researcher for a specific research project. These data are collected by directly asking specific questions. The two principal research methodologies that can be used to obtain primary data are quantitative research and qualitative research.

- *Quantitative research* is conducted to obtain statistically valid numerical data projectable to a larger population. It usually involves a large number of people to gather broad, generalizable results. Data collection methods range from telephone surveys and direct mail questionnaires to consumer panels and intercept studies. The intent is to survey as many people as deemed appropriate to gain statistical information that can be used to answer pertinent questions.

- *Qualitative research* provides a greater understanding of perceptions, opinions, attitudes and behavior patterns. It generally entails discussions with a small group of people to gather in-depth explanatory data that are interpretive and descriptive. The intent is to talk to fewer people—typically on a one-on-one basis or through focus groups—about their opinions, perceptions and beliefs.

A broad range of qualitative research methods are available to meet specific research needs:

- Focus groups
  - Full size, minis or triads
  - Online/teleconferencing
  - Focus panels

- Personal interviews
  - One-on-ones or dyads
  - At home/work
  - In plant/store

- Observational assessments
  - Mystery shopper programs
  - Customer-service call monitoring
  - Sales call observation
  - Employee training evaluation

Focus groups and in-depth interviews are the more frequently used qualitative methodologies. Focus groups are typically made up of eight to ten respondents, and a group discussion is ideally moderated by a specialist in qualitative research. Sessions typically last two hours, and not all respondents answer every question. In-depth interviews involve only one individual with a moderator or interviewer and can last anywhere from thirty minutes to an hour. The interviewees answer each of the moderator's questions in detail, and the moderator may probe further for in-depth responses.

Both quantitative and qualitative data can be used to meet specific research project objectives. Figure 3 presents a comparison between quantitative research and qualitative research approaches.

	Quantitive	Qualitative
Purpose	Predict	Describe
Description	Objective/statistical—what and how many	Subjective/interpretive—how and why
Form	Standardized measures Predetermined response categories	Nonstandard measures Open–ended questioning
Sample	Large number of people—randomly selected	Small group of people—specifically selected
Result	Broad, generalizable data—understanding of group similarities and patterns	In-depth exploratory information—understanding of individual differences and patterns
Strengths	Statistically reliable	Illustrative explanations, detailed information, variable content

Figure 3.   Comparison of research approaches

The features of quantitative and qualitative research methods are highlighted in Figures 4 and 5.

Secondary data–those which already exist and are available from another source–can be particularly valuable in examining industry trends, demographic and psychographic information and market segmentation. These data can include information from an organization's detailed database, published reference material and syndicated sources of information.

When selecting the appropriate research methodology, an issue to consider is whether any useful data already exist. Then, the scope of the research effort (e.g., current customers, non-customers, former customers, employees, former employees, geographic boundaries) must be covered. Additional fact-finding questions about the target respondents (e.g., demographic information,

	Direct Mail Surveys	Telephone Surveys	Personal Interviews
Cost per interview	Least expensive	Moderately expensive	Most expensive
Speed of data collection	Slowest	Fastest	Moderately slow
Quantity of information	Moderate	Least	Most
Flexibility of interview process	Least	Moderate	Most
Geographical dispersion of interviewees	Very broad	Broad	Limited
Refusals or nonresponse rate	Greatest	Moderate	Least
Perceived anonymity of respondents	High	Moderate	Low

Figure 4. Features of quantitative research

	Focus Groups	In-depth Interviews
Number of respondents	Eight to ten per group	One individual (at a time)
Ideally used when	Group influence is desirable Timing is critical Efficent data collection is needed	Group influence is undesirable Legal restrictions or confidentiality issues exist Subject is intimate or sensitive
Results achieved	Insight into attitudes, beliefs, opinions and perceptions	In-depth detailed responses
Benefits	Efficient data collection Rapid turnaround time Comments can be heard by observers	No group biases Deeper probing into specific issues Can be conducted almost anywhere
Limitations	Possible group bias Requires special research facility More expensive than survey research	Higher cost per interview Takes more time than focus groups Higher risk of interviewee problems

Figure 5. Features of qualitative research

age, gender, income, marital status, education level and occupation) and issues pertaining to the research budget and project schedules then need to be addressed. Once the specific research objectives and the overall business goals are understood, the proper methodology (or combination of methods) can be selected. The next step is to implement the research initiative.

Performing the Research

As with any other successful business project, the research initiative needs to be monitored and supervised to ensure the integrity of the data collection process. Suppliers (such as focus group facilities, moderators, telephone interviewers, questionnaire writers, data analysts and research consultants) should be selected based on qualifications and experience. In addition, competitive issues and organizational ideals should be considered to avoid any potential conflicts.

Depending on the nature of the research project, the following phases generally take place:

- Planning and preparation
  - Define the research purpose and objectives
  - Develop the project plan (methodology, scope, location and so on)
  - Schedule interviews or focus groups
  - Prepare the screener or questionnaire and recruiting instructions

- Field Work
  - Recruit and validate respondents
  - Conduct interviews or focus groups

- Reporting
  - Compile findings
  - Analyze results
  - Develop report
  - Present findings

Focus group projects (qualitative research) typically entail the following steps:

1. Initial contact: The research supplier meets with the client to define the research objectives.

2. Proposal: The supplier prepares a summary of the proposed approach, methodology, location, schedule and costs.

3. Proposal acceptance: The client agrees on the scope, budget and terms.

4. Recruitment screener: The supplier prepares a list of specifications to be used in recruiting participants. Specifications typically include the target age-group, gender, income bracket, product preferences and other screening criteria.

5. Moderator's discussion guide: The supplier prepares an outline of the focus group session, from the introduction and warm-up, to various discussion points and the closing. The guide also defines materials and concepts (e.g., product, brand, packaging, image, alternatives).

6. Report: The supplier presents the client with a summary of research findings, in the form of a debriefing or a presentation, a top-of-mind summary or a full report.

Questionnaires (quantitative research) usually address the following considerations:

- Background: What information is required, who are the target respondents, what method of communication will be used to obtain the required information?

- Format: Questions can be open-ended or close-ended (e.g., multiple choices). Respondents can be asked to place items on a scale of one to ten, for example, or to rank items in order of importance or in sequential order.

- Layout: The questionnaire should be clear and logical, with minimal opportunity for incorrect interpretations or wrong assumptions.

It is very important to thoroughly and objectively critique and pretest any questionnaire before actually using it.

Using the Findings

Because the approach to qualitative research is fairly subjective, the findings may be somewhat interpretive. The information gathered in focus groups or in-depth interviews is most meaningful, and best used, for insight and direction as it deals mainly with how and why individuals feel the way they do about a product or service. However, quantitative research is more objective because the findings are statistical in nature. The analysis focuses on how many respondents answer the questions a certain way. Furthermore, the data collected from a telephone or mail survey are predictable and projectable to a population larger than the one studied.

Depending on the chosen methodology, decision makers should use either the descriptive (qualitative) findings or the predictive (quantitative) findings. In either event, analysis provides the basis for an action plan for enhancing customer satisfaction. It is a waste of valuable time, money and resources to plan, implement and perform a market research study without acting on the findings. The most effective research presentations include not just an in-depth analysis of the data, but specific recommendations for follow-up action. Only if such action is taken can the organization continuously improve. If a research project does not provide the decision maker with actionable information, or if action is not taken on the findings, then the value of the research effort is lost.

IV.

PROCESS MANAGEMENT

*America's economic strength relies first and foremost
on our ability to innovate—through technology,
managerial commitment, and labor's skill—
and to improve productivity and quality.*

Ronald Reagan

With an effective quality system in place and an appropriate customer focus environment established, the organization is now best prepared to deploy process management techniques. Management's commitment is the first step to instilling a *quality awareness* throughout the organization. Total quality approaches can then be instituted with the effective use of *process analysis* techniques and timely *quality planning*.

Quality Awareness

In today's competitive environment, an effective *total quality management system* must be an organized, structured and institutionalized approach for conducting a business—with the ultimate goal of continuous improvement and meeting or exceeding customer expectations. To be successful, the system requires a commitment by management, strategic quality planning, a drive for continuous improvement and relevant performance measurement. All employees—not just those that build the product or provide the services—should be involved. The focus should be on both the internal customers (those within the organization) as well as the external customers (those outside the company—from the initial recipient to the end-users of the product or service). In assessing the adequacy of an organization's quality management system, several critical ingredients could be considered (see Figure 6).

Management Involvement

Top management must play a leading role in defining the company's quality policy and operational philosophy. Management should proactively participate in the strategic and quality planning process and then support both long- and short-term quality and service improvement plans by providing appropriate resources for their successful deployment. Improvement projects should be encouraged and teams should be supported. Periodic reviews should be held to assure that established goals and milestones are being accomplished.

Employee Participation

All employees should be aware of, and involved in, the organization's quality improvement initiatives. They should have the opportunity to receive training on the appropriate tools and skills necessary to perform their jobs effectively. Consistent with the organization's culture, members of the work force should be empowered to exercise discretion pertaining to service, quality and customer-related issues in their functional areas.

Management Involvement
- Policy and plans
- Resources
- Project teams
- Status reviews
- Lead by example

Employee Participation
- All employees
- Training
- Empowered teams/ work groups
- Process improvement projects

Customer Focus
- External customers
- Internal customers
- Requirements
- Expectations

Strategic Planning
- Short- and long-term
- Total quality business plan
- Goals and objectives
- Performance measurement

Process Control
- Operational analysis
- Process mapping
- Statistical process control
- Consistency
- Capability
- Process improvement

Problem Solving
- Analytical techniques
- Root cause corrective action
- Management participation

Performance Measurement
- Goals/objectives
- Plans
- Measures/indicators
- Linkage to customer satisfaction
- Results monitoring

Quality Cost Visibility
- Prevention
- Appraisal
- Internal failure
- External failure
- Other key financial indicators

Education and Training
- Training plan
- On-the-job training
- Quality awareness
- Process analysis
- Skills enhancement
- Customer relations
- Effectiveness evaluation

Supplier Partnerships
- Qualification
- Commitment
  - Quality
  - Delivery
  - Price
- Partnerships or alliances

Attention to Detail
- Dedication
- Logic and common sense
- Continuous improvement

Figure 6. ***Essential for business improvement***

Customer Focus

Throughout the organization, every employee should clearly understand the requirements and expectations of their customers. External customer requirements and expectations should be systematically determined and defined. Internally, within the organization, each employee should recognize the needs of his or her immediate customers. The entire work force should strive for achieving and exceeding customer satisfaction.

Strategic Planning

The quality business plan should be derived from–and linked with–the company's strategic business plan. Both short- and long-term goals and objectives should be clearly defined with measurable milestones and assigned responsibilities. Expectations and deliverables should also be defined to establish the framework for meaningful measurement of performance and monitoring of accomplishments.

Process Control

Depending on the nature of the organization, effective process controls should be in place. After appropriate analysis, processes should be mapped, illustrated with a flowchart and documented with useful procedures and work instructions. Where applicable, appropriate statistical process control methods should be used to assure process consistency and capability. Process performance parameters and indicators should be monitored so that performance improvement measures can be assessed.

Problem Solving

Appropriate analytical techniques should be used to address and resolve problems. Fundamental root causes should be identified and eliminated. Management should actively oversee the corrective action process to assure effectiveness of the problem-solving and close-out process. Chapter 5 introduces several powerful problem-solving tools.

Performance Measurement

Appropriate product, process and organization measures should be monitored. These measures should be linked to the company's key business factors and strategic planning parameters—and deployed and translated vertically throughout the organization. To be most effective, performance indicators should be linked to relevant customer satisfaction criteria. Performance levels should be communicated among all employees that participate in, contribute to or influence the performance results. This employee involvement, along with management's participation, will positively affect—and drive—performance improvement. Chapter 6 highlights the important linkage of key performance measures.

Quality Cost Visibility

A very powerful business improvement indicator, the organization's costs of quality should be defined and tracked. Quality costs conventionally include preventive, appraisal and internal and external failure costs. When compared with traditional measures (e.g., manufacturing costs, cost of goods sold or, better yet, percent profit), quality costs are usually a substantial proportion—typically as much as 15 to 20 percent of sales. The high cost of waste can provide the motivation and direction for business performance improvement.

Education and Training

The organization's training plan should provide for an appropriate analysis of training needs as well as a means of determining and assuring the effectiveness of training provided. The nature and scope of employee education and training should include quality awareness, process analysis and improvement tools, special skills enhancement and customer relationships. Training should extend to meaningful on-the-job applications for all types and categories of employees.

Supplier Partnerships

Effective vendor relations are becoming more and more important in today's competitive environment. In looking toward the long-term, world-class organizations are strengthening the nature of their alliances or partnerships with key suppliers. Consistent with the expectations or projections for ongoing business, the expectations for quality, delivery and price are being defined and agreed upon for such longer-term relationships.

Attention to Detail

A final ingredient in the organization's checklist for an effective total quality management system is the striving for attention to detail. If it is important to perform a task or achieve a goal, that task or goal should be documented—and complied with. If it is not important, time should not be wasted and attention should stay focused on those elements critical for the business success.

Total Quality Management

Over the past several years, a lot has been written—and much has been done—on the subject of total quality management (TQM). TQM could be considered both a philosophy and a management process with two dimensions: cultural and technical. Although TQM involves all employees, management must actively lead the initiative in a continuous effort to improve business systems and processes by focusing on customers and meeting their requirements. As an overview of this very powerful concept, the next three sections look briefly at approaches taken by some Malcolm Baldrige National Quality Award winners.

Ames Rubber Corporation. Ames produces rubber rollers used in office machines and other highly specialized parts. Ames has adopted the basic principle of total quality, that is, providing its internal and external customers with innovative products and services that fully satisfy their requirements. Total quality improvement and the achievement of excellence is the job of every Ames employee or "teammate." In characterizing the concepts of total quality, Ames has changed its conventional view of "quality (q)" (which has been centered around inspection and an allowable level of defects) to "Total Quality

(TQ)" (which means conformance to customer requirements, both internal and external) as follows:

- Performance standard: Consistently meeting customer requirements—not "close enough" or "almost."

- System: Knowing customer requirements and preventing mistakes from happening—not only finding and fixing mistakes.

- Selection of opportunity: Looking for quality improvement areas with the greatest payback (e.g., cost of nonconformance).

- Measurement of performance: Measuring our work against customer requirements—not opinions or guesses.

- Responsibility: Quality improvement is the responsibility of every teammate—not just the quality department.

ADAC Laboratories. In establishing its TQM approach, ADAC, a Silicon Valley–based maker of high-technology health-care products, has defined a companywide "language of quality" and a set of concepts and practices for enhancing customer satisfaction. ADAC has adopted a set of TQM Principles used in all of its activities:

Focus on Customers
1. Customers come first—Our primary obligation is to exceed the expectations of our customers. Customer satisfaction is the best and only lasting means of achieving business success.

Continuous Improvement

2. Management by fact—The discovery and analysis of facts is the basis of systematic problem solving, continuous improvement and decision making.

3. Management by process—Focus on process improvement to achieve results. Management by process requires first standardizing the methods and processes by which we do work and then continuously improving our processes.

4. Continuous improvement—Systematic and iterative application of the PDCA (Plan-Do-Check-Act) cycle to achieve customer satisfaction and business success.

5. Focus on the vital few—Focus on those activities which make a big difference in the company's quality and performance.

Total Company Participation

6. Everyone participates—All employees are expected to continuously improve the processes by which we do our jobs using TQM methods.

7. Management leadership of TQM—Management must be committed to TQM and must lead by example.

8. Respect for individuals—We must listen with empathy, treat each other as customers and trust each other.

9. Teamwork—Many problems are better solved by people working in teams than by people working individually.

Mutual Learning
10. Mutual learning–TQM begins and ends with education. Mutual learning accelerates the rate of improvement.

AT&T. AT&T's Total Quality Approach has been used to manage its businesses with ever-increasing efficiency and effectiveness (see Figure 7).

AT&T employees continues to be guided by their fundamental principles:

- The customer comes first.

- Quality happens through people.

- All work is part of a process.

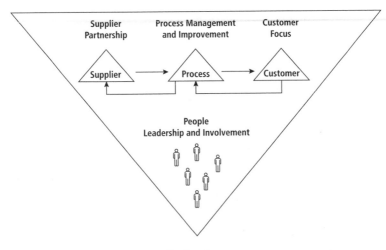

Figure 7. AT&T's Total Quality Approach
Reproduced with the permission of AT&T © 1992. All rights reserved.

- Suppliers are an integral part of our business.

- Prevention is achieved through planning.

- Quality improvement never ends.

Process Analysis

Process analysis entails a logical approach to understanding a process, defining and analyzing its elements (activities and tasks) and improving its effectiveness. A process can be defined as the people, procedures, machines and material organized into work activities to make a product or provide a service. A process can be effectively analyzed by defining inputs from suppliers and outputs to customers, understanding supplier and customer expectations, and assessing performance. In such an analysis, the following questions can be addressed:

- What are the process steps?

- Who are the customers?

- Who are the suppliers?

- What are the process inputs and outputs?

- What are their requirements and expectations?

- How is performance measured?

- How can performance be improved?

The answers to these questions can facilitate the typical steps in a process analysis:

1. Identify the process scope, functions and interrelationships.

2. Establish process ownership.

3. Determine customer requirements.

4. Define supplier interfaces.

5. Map the process (using flowcharts, input/output analysis and performance measurement).

6. Collect current process performance data and results.

7. Rate the process (in terms of control and capability).

8. Analyze the process (by brainstorming, cause-and-effect analysis and root cause analysis).

9. Benchmark the process (see Quality Improvement Tools in Chapter 5).

10. Plan and prioritize process changes.

11. Develop improvement plans.

12. Establish performance goals or targets.

13. Implement improvement solutions.

Process mapping entails the development of a flowchart (or process map). Process flowcharts delineate the process inputs, activities, decision points and outputs. Using flowcharts, companies investigating opportunities for improvement can gain a detailed understanding of how the process actually works, uncover potential sources of trouble and identify unnecessary steps in the process. Flowcharts can be applied to any aspect of the process—from the flow of material and product to the steps in providing a service, such as sales, forecasting, issue of purchase orders and invoice processing. Typical process flowchart symbols are shown in Figure 8.

Traditional steps in developing the flowchart are shown in Figure 9.

A useful checklist for analyzing the process is shown in Figure 10.

A variety of tools are available to facilitate process improvement. Problem solving and some of the most popular quality improvement tools are introduced in Chapter 5.

Quality Planning

Quality planning can be defined as a structured method of defining and establishing the steps necessary to ensure that a product or service satisfies the customer. When properly performed in a timely manner, quality planning can facilitate the identification of necessary resources, promote the early identification of required changes and help provide the quality or service on-time and cost-effectively. Needless to say, meaningful quality planning should take place well in advance of actual production/launch, that is, during the early planning phase (when the product concept is initiated and the program is defined and approved) and the design and development phase (when the product and

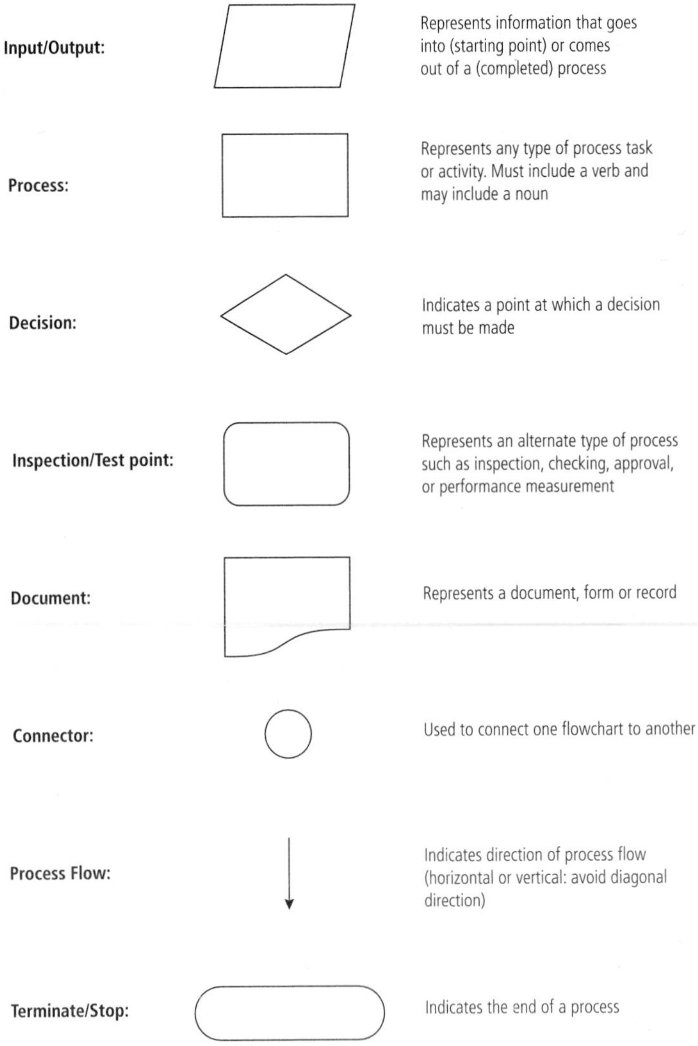

Input/Output:		Represents information that goes into (starting point) or comes out of a (completed) process
Process:		Represents any type of process task or activity. Must include a verb and may include a noun
Decision:		Indicates a point at which a decision must be made
Inspection/Test point:		Represents an alternate type of process such as inspection, checking, approval, or performance measurement
Document:		Represents a document, form or record
Connector:		Used to connect one flowchart to another
Process Flow:		Indicates direction of process flow (horizontal or vertical: avoid diagonal direction)
Terminate/Stop:		Indicates the end of a process

Figure 8.   Flowchart symbols

1. Identify the input to the process or activity.
2. For each input, ask questions such as:
   - Who supplies the input?
   - Who receives the input?
   - What is the first thing that is done with the input?
3. List the outputs from the process or activity.
4. For each output, ask questions such as:
   - Who receives this output?
   - What are the requirements or expectations?
5. Use the appropriate flowchart symbols to show activities and decisions involved in converting the inputs to outputs (i.e., develop the process).
6. Review and, if necessary, rework the chart in terms of:
   - Proper work/information flow
   - Serial and parallel nature of the activities
   - Rework loops and special paths for ad-hoc procedures
   - High repeating loops
   - All major decision points
   - Accurate capture of what really happens
   - Inputs from other processes that depict outputs to this chart
7. Date the chart. It should serve as a record of the current process.

Figure 9.   Developing the flowchart

process designs are developed and verified, prototypes are produced and tested and the product and processes are validated).

Several factors should be considered before the preliminary planning stage, including input from the customer (or potential customers), the company's business plan and marketing strategy, product and process benchmark data, reliability data and business assumptions. The major phases of a typical project/product quality planning process are shown in Figure 11.

1. Identify "high repeat" loops
2. Challenge all decision points.
   - Are they needed?
   - Are alternate paths necessary? Clear?
3. Can paths be run in parallel?
4. Do all "in-out" connecting points between process flowcharts agree?
5. Ask "what if" questions.
   - Drop out a loop: What happens?
   - Eliminate certain steps (activities): What happens?
6. What are the value-adding steps? The non-value-adding steps?
7. How can non-value-adding steps be reduced or eliminated?
8. What are the throughput times?
9. What are the touch times (actual work)?
10. Which activities take the longest?
11. Determine what holds up throughput.
    - Information?
    - Material?
    - Inputs from another process flow path?
12. Which activities are most critical—or cause the most damage if they fail?

Figure 10. Analyzing the process

At the end of the design and development phase, a variety of outputs should be available prior to production, such as:

- Design parameters and reliability goals
- Failure mode and effects analyses (FMEAs) of product design

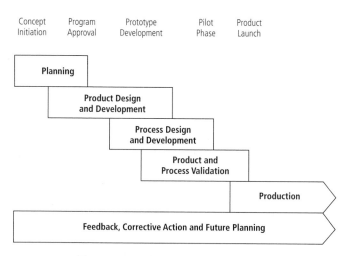

Concept Initiation Program Approval Prototype Development Pilot Phase Product Launch

Figure 11.   Quality planning phases

- Process FMEAs

- Bills of materials and engineering drawings

- Identified special product characteristics and critical process parameters

- Material/process/packaging specifications

- Manufacturing, assembly and quality assurance plans

- Equipment, tooling and gauging requirements

- Inspection, test and control plans

- Work instructions

Two powerful tools are useful for meaningful quality planning: FMEAs and control plans.

Failure Mode and Effect Analysis

FMEA is a systematic and disciplined analytical technique to address potential and known product, process or system failure modes. FMEAs help in identifying the causes and effects of each failure mode; understanding the failure mechanisms; prioritizing the identified failure modes according to frequency of occurrence, severity and detection ability; and providing the means for problem elimination and corrective action follow-up.

FMEAs can be used effectively for both processes (PFMEA) and product designs (DFMEA). In either instance, the impact of a potential failure is analyzed with respect to the failure's estimated frequency of occurrence, the severity of the failure and the likelihood of detecting the failure. Using a scale of one to ten, a *risk priority number* is calculated for each identified potential failure mode, and appropriate actions are instituted to minimize the probability of such a failure.

Control Plans

Control Plans provide a structured approach for the identification and implementation of methods to control the product or process characteristics, minimize variation and address any out-of-control situations that may arise. A control plan will not replace detailed work instructions; however, it will describe actions necessary to ensure that the process is maintained in a state of control consistent with the prescribed measurement system to avoid nonconformity of products. Control plans are usually developed by multidisciplinary teams to maximize process knowledge and understanding.

Under the auspices of the Automotive Industry Action Group (AIAG), the automotive sector's "Big Three" (Chrysler Corporation, Ford Motor Company and General Motors Corporation) have developed a useful publication titled *Advanced Product Quality Planning and Control Plan* (APQP). Copies can be obtained from the AIAG (see address on page 23).

V.

QUALITY IMPROVEMENT

*The improvement of quality in products and
the improvement of quality in service—these
are national priorities as never before.*

George Bush

With the appropriate conducive-to-change climate in place, the organization is now ready to institute and deploy a results-oriented quality improvement process—by selectively choosing from, and using, a variety of available quality improvement tools and techniques.

The Quality Improvement Process

Before implementing any quality improvement process, it is important to consider and understand basic quality or service issues:

- How is the quality or service defined?

- What is the operational system?

- What are the performance standards?

- How is quality or service measured?

Quality improvement could be defined as a management process consisting of the following typical steps:

1. Define the organization's vision, values, policy and mission

2. Identify specific improvement actions

3. Establish project priorities

4. Motivate the workforce by empowering teams

5. Foster an atmosphere of participative management

6. Develop the quality business plan

7. Provide necessary education and training

8. Analyze processes

9. Measure performance

10. Establish performance measurement linkages

11. Commit to improvement

12. Evaluate results

13. Achieve continuous improvement

To deploy an effective problem-solving and improvement process, the stage must be set within the organization. Throughout the world, the Plan, Do, Check, Act (PDCA) cycle has been portrayed as an operational model for a logical quality improvement process (see Figure 12).

The popularized problem-solving process can be described as follows:

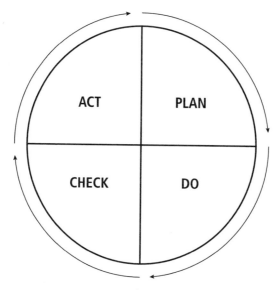

Figure 12. **The PDCA cycle**

- Plan: Identify the specific, prioritized problem; determine how much information is available; observe and analyze; establish a plan to isolate the causes and plan corrective actions

- Do: Obtain data; apply and carry out the test or experiment

- Check: Verify and evaluate results and observe the effects of the test; compare with established goals

- Act: Determine what was learned; ascertain what can be changed; and prepare for and act on the next phases of action

Many organizations have amplified and refined the classical PDCA cycle into a more detailed quality improvement process. The following sections describe how some companies have done so.

Alcoa. Alcoa has adopted an Eight-Step Quality Improvement Process designed to seek opportunities to increase customer satisfaction and solve problems that limit performance:

1. Define problems and quality improvement opportunities.

2. Select the problem or opportunity

3. Analyze causes and effects

4. Generate potential actions

5. Evaluate and select actions

6. Test effectiveness of actions

7. Implement

8. Monitor

AT&T. Throughout AT&T[1], many cross-functional teams are managing and improving processes following its Process Quality Management and Improvement (PQMI)[1] methodology:

1. Establish process management responsibilities

2. Baseline the current process and identify customer requirements

---

1   Adapted from the original with permission of AT&T © 1992. All rights reserved.

3. Define and establish measures

4. Assess conformance to customer requirements

5. Investigate to find improvement opportunities

6. Rank the opportunities and set objectives

7. Continuously improve the process

Ames Rubber Corporation. Ames Rubber Corporation (a Baldrige winner) has deployed a Six-Step Problem-Solving Process (PSP):

1. Identify and select problem

2. Analyze problem

3. Generate potential solutions

4. Select and plan solution

5. Implement solution

6. Evaluate solution

Ames has augmented their problem-solving process with a Nine-Step Quality Improvement Process (QIP):

1. Identify output (What do I produce?)

2. Identify customer (Who do I produce it for?)

3. Identify customer requirements (What does the customer need, want, expect?)

4. Translate requirements into supplier specifications (What do the requirements mean to me?)

5. Identify steps in work process (How will I make it?)

6. Select measurements (How will I know I am succeeding?)

7. Determine process capability (Will this work process enable me to produce an output that satisfies customer requirements? If not, use the PSP.)

8. Evaluate results (Are changes required in the process? Where are there additional opportunities for quality improvement? Use the PSP.)

9. Recycle (How could this output be produced more efficiently?)

AT&T's Transmission Systems Business Unit. The Transmission Systems Business Unit of AT&T's Networking Systems Group (a Baldrige winner) uses seven steps for quality improvement and problem solving:

1. Reason for improvement: Identify a theme (problem) and the reason for working on it

2. Current situation: Select a problem and set a target for improvement

3. Analysis: Identify and verify the root causes of the problem

4. Countermeasures: Plan and implement countermeasures that will correct the root causes of the problem

5. Results: Confirm that the problem and its root causes have been decreased and the target for improvement has been met

6. Standardization: Prevent the problem and its root causes from recurring

7. Future plans: Plan what to do about any remaining problems and evaluate the team's effectiveness

Eastman Chemical Company. Eastman Chemical Company (a Baldrige winner) has deployed a team-oriented Quality Management Process (QMP) that provides a common framework and language for continual improvement:

- Customer focus: The QMP begins and ends with Eastman's customers.

- Assess organization: Each team assesses who its customers are, why it exists and what it must do to be successful.

- Plan improvement: Teams select improvement areas that are directly linked to their customers' needs and the company's objectives.

- Do improvement: Project teams use logic and data—with both a diagnostic and remedial journey—to identify and eliminate problems in existing processes or design and implement new processes.

- Check and act: The team evaluates the performance of the new or improved processes. Other actions, such as standardization, root cause determination, corrective action, and positive reinforcement are also initiated.

Ford Motor Company's Powertrain Operations. Ford Motor Company's Powertrain Operations has deployed a team-oriented problem-solving process using the Eight-Discipline (8-D) approach (see Figure 13).

GTE Directories Corporation. GTE Directories Corporation (a Baldrige winner) has defined quality as "anticipating, understanding and meeting or exceeding customers' needs in an effective, efficient manner that is beneficial to both parties." Four key factors characterize GTE's Quality Improvement Journey:

- Customer-driven management that bases all business decisions on customer needs and expectations determined through solid quantitative and qualitative research

- Malcolm Baldrige National Quality Award criteria and methodology as a framework for examination and improvement

- Formal quality improvement processes, including infrastructure, tools, techniques, training, motivation, tracking and quality improvement management

- Cross-functional team-based management focused on processes and goals rather than functional protocols

IBM. IBM has instituted a five-stage problem-solving process (see Figure 14).

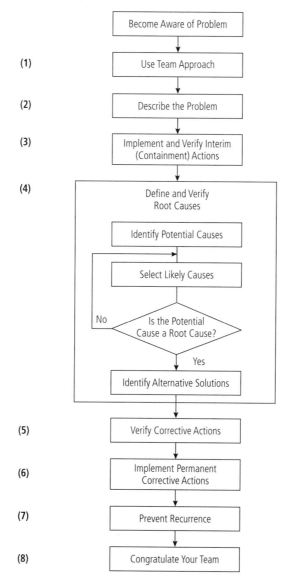

Figure 13.   Ford's problem-solving process
Copyright 1987, Ford Motor Company. Used with permission

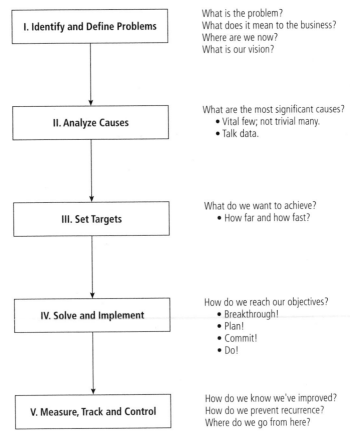

Figure 14. *IBM's five-stage problem-solving process*
Used with permission.

Creating Problem Statements

When solving problems, many organizations frequently do not adequately solve (or even address) the real problem. To keep the main problem in focus, it is helpful to first develop an appropriate *problem statement*. A problem statement should clarify and detail the planned actions necessary to fulfill the mission or project objective. A proper problem statement facilitates focus on the real issues.

As prescribed by Alcoa, a problem statement should explicitly and clearly explain the situation to be addressed:

- State the specifics of the problem or opportunity

- Describe the effect of the problem or the anticipated gain from the opportunity

- Identify some measure of the problem

- Focus on the gap between what is and what should (could) be

- Do not imply or present a solution

- The statement should be positively worded and not state the problem as a question

- Avoid broad general terms such as quality, productivity and communication

- State why the situation is important

Legend has it that Albert Einstein was once asked how would he spend his time if some imminent disaster threatened the world and he had one hour to save it. Einstein thought for a minute and then replied that he "would spend the first fifty-five minutes identifying the problem and the last five minutes solving it." The development of a meaningful problem statement should be considered a prerequisite before embarking on the solution.

Identifying Barriers and Enablers

To facilitate effective problem solving, it is useful to identify *barriers* and *enablers:*

- Barriers: the many obstacles to achieving change and making desired improvements

- Enablers: the items in place that will assist and support efforts to change and make the needed improvements

Defining the Root Cause

To effectively solve and eliminate a problem, the true *root cause* should be determined. The root cause is the most basic reason for an undesirable condition or problem, which, if eliminated or corrected, would have prevented the problem from occurring or recurring. Root cause analysis efforts often fail because they cannot clearly distinguish between apparent and root causes. (*Apparent causes* usually represent the immediate or obvious reason for a problem.) If only the symptoms or apparent causes are treated, then the problem or fault is very likely to recur. Corrective actions can resolve the apparent cause, but only when the real reason for the problem (the *root cause*) is identified and treated can the recurrence be prevented (see Figure 15).

One very effective way to determine the real root cause of a problem is by performing what is called the Five-Why Analysis. When addressing the problem, ask "Why did it happen?" Then, in response to that answer,

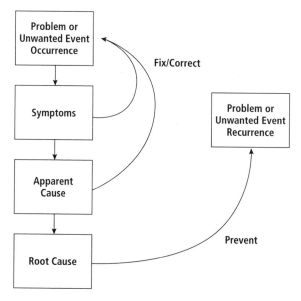

Figure 15.   Root cause analysis

Adapted from Wilson, Dell, and Anderson, Root Cause Analysis, *ASQ Quality Press, Milwaukee, 1993. Used with permission.*

ask "Why did that happen?" Again, ask "Why?" Repeat this sequence until no further answers can be determined (typically four to six times). The result should be the most deep-rooted, highest-level root cause of the problem. This technique is very powerful.

Quality Improvement Tools

As part of the improvement process, a variety of classical quality or performance improvement tools are extensively used, including benchmarking, brainstorming, cause-and-effect analysis, data collection techniques, Pareto analysis, process reengineering, statistical methods, teamwork and empowerment.

Benchmarking

Benchmarking can be defined as the "search for industry best practices that lead to superior performance." The Xerox Corporation is recognized as the pioneer of the benchmarking process. Its model has been adopted throughout the world. The proper benchmarking steps, when fully integrated into processes, can lead to attainment of a performance leadership position (see Figure 16).

Brainstorming

Brainstorming is an idea-generating technique that typically uses the mental capacity of a group of people and encourages creative thinking. Individuals present their ideas so that others have the opportunity to build on them. Popular brainstorming methods include "free wheeling," "round-robin," and the use of written submissions.

Cause-and-Effect Analysis

Cause-and-effect analysis offers a systematic way of looking at a specific effect (or problem) and identifying its potential causes. Also referred to as fishbone diagrams (because of their shape) or Ishikawa diagrams (named after Dr. Kaoru Ishikawa, the Japanese statistician), the cause-and-effect diagram is a useful analysis and improvement tool.

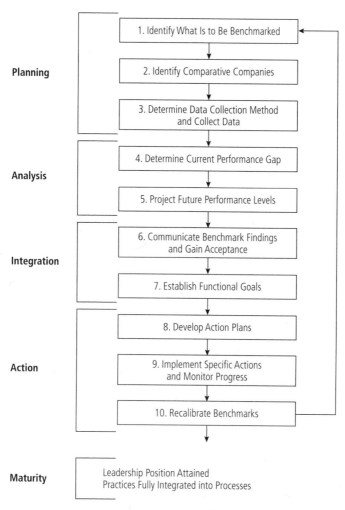

Figure 16.   Benchmarking process

Adapted from Camp, Benchmarking, ASQ Quality Press,
Milwaukee, 1989. Used with permission.

Data Collection Techniques

Data collection techniques provide the foundation for information accuracy, credibility and analysis. Some of the more common data capture and display methods include:

- Check sheets (to collect and record data)

- Histograms (to show frequency of occurrence over intervals of measured values)

- Run charts (to graphically portray chronological performance levels)

- Scatter diagrams (to recognize correlation or cause-and-effect relationships)

Pareto Analysis

Pareto analysis entails a graphical plot that ranks the distribution of items by frequency of occurrence. It is used to focus attention on the most critical or severe issues, problems or opportunities (the "vital few") while showing the remaining ("trivial many") in descending order.

Process Reengineering

Process reengineering is a powerful business improvement tool that enables an organization to make major improvements in processing time (cycle or throughput), costs and customer satisfaction. It focuses on improving key business processes that are critical to the success of the business.

Statistical Methods

Statistical methods entail a logical mentality that recognizes and understands variation—particularly the difference between common causes (those inherent in the process) and special causes (intermittent, sometimes called assignable causes). A process can be determined to be in a state of statistical control (or stable) when all special causes have been eliminated and only common causes remain. *Control charts,* when used properly, are a very powerful tool to focus on variation and determine level of control (stability) of the process. Two basic types of control charts depend on the type of data being monitored or the nature of the process measure: *variables* (e.g., averages, ranges, standard deviation, individuals and moving ranges) and *attributes* (fraction rejected or proportion nonconforming, number of nonconforming items, number of nonconformities and number of nonconformities per unit). *Process capability* can be defined as the ability of a process to meet specifications or to operate at a level that is acceptable to the customer or user. *Six Sigma Quality* is a term that was popularized in the 1990s to denote a very high performance level of virtually zero defects—specifically, when a process is generating no more than three or four defects (i.e., errors, late deliveries and so on) per million items/units processed.

Teams and Empowerment

Teams consist of people working together toward a common goal with a common mission and purpose. When used effectively, teams have a broader perspective and consider more alternatives than do individuals. They also bring ownership to the outcome, accumulate more facts and provide for greater participation and growth opportunities for employees. There are many different types of teams such as customer/supplier, task/project, lead/management, cross-functional, natural work groups and self-governing work teams. *Empowerment* is the process of giving employees greater degrees of responsibility, authority and accountability to manage work at their level. Levels of empowerment are influenced by the organization's culture, management style and employee comfort.

Other Tools and Techniques

A variety of other improvement tools and techniques, such as affinity diagrams, force-field analysis, KAIZEN, multivoting, quality function deployment and simultaneous engineering, are also available to the problem solver:

- *Affinity diagrams* are used to compile and organize a number of ideas, opinions and observations into logical relationships between items. Affinity diagrams provide a clear perspective of large and complex problems.

- *Force-field analysis* recognizes that *driving forces* facilitate change while *restraining forces* impede forward progress. By graphically tabulating those forces side by side, the analysis can help recognize the competing forces and strengthen the positive factors, while reducing the negative resistance to desired change.

- The essence of the *KAIZEN* (a trademark of the KAIZEN Institute, Ltd.) philosophy is that constant improvement is a way of life, that is, small improvements made in the status quo as a result of ongoing efforts. Innovation, on the other hand, involves a drastic improvement as a result of investments in new technology, equipment or resources. KAIZEN involves everyone in the management hierarchy, including top management, middle management, staff, supervisors and workers.

- *Multivoting* (or nominal group technique) enables a group or team to select what they consider to be the most important problem, idea or solution. By individually ranking the issues, multivoting allows a consensus priority to be determined.

- *Quality function deployment* (QFD) is a process for converting the voice of the customer into specific quality elements and operational requirements. Commonly referred to as the *house of quality,* QFD logically links and graphically translates customer attributes to engineering characteristics, part characteristics, process operations and production requirements.

- *Simultaneous or concurrent engineering* allows for a faster product-design cycle because the needs and requirements of all functions (e.g., customers, engineers, suppliers and manufacturing) are considered early in the conceptual, design and development stages. The conceptual *1/10/100 rule* recognizes that an input or change made (to prevent a defect) early in the development phase would cost one-tenth of the cost to institute that change later in the cycle, and one-hundredth of the cost if the defect is detected and addressed only much later in the production process.

For those readers interested in additional details on the use and application of these techniques, a bibliography is provided at the end of this book.

VI.

PERFORMANCE MEASUREMENT

*When you can measure what you are speaking about, and you
express it in numbers, you know something about it. But when
you cannot measure it, when you cannot express it in numbers,
your knowledge is of a meager and unsatisfactory kind.*

Lord Kelvin, 1883

T he cornerstone of any improvement process is
the performance measurement system. In many
organizations, a lot of energy and resources are
devoted to measuring performance—but not always of the
right things. To be most relevant and useful, key measures
or indicators should directly or indirectly relate to the key
business factors, that is, those measures that are predictors
of business success or customer satisfaction. This requires
a *linkage* between key business factors and the critical processes of the business—the integration of service and quality goals into the business strategic and tactical planning
cycles—and the involvement of all employees in improving
performance. The effective closing of any identified gaps,
reflected in key performance measures and indicators,
must be part of the business strategic planning and continuous improvement processes.

Quality planning must be a part of the business planning process that integrates policy deployment, control, and performance monitoring (both financial and nonfinancial results). Business plans and quality and service strategies are inseparable.

Linkage of Performance Measures

In dealing with performance measurement (of the right measures), there are many types of linkages:

- Vertical linkage of process parameters and departmental indicators up to the business unit level

- Linkage of predictors of customer satisfaction with appropriate customer satisfaction measures

- Linkage of financial indicators to quality and service performance measures

Effective linkage of appropriate performance measures is critical to achieving superior business results and competitive advantage. This linkage is clearly reflected in the Malcolm Baldrige National Quality Award Criteria for Performance Excellence. The scoring and feedback of applicant responses are based on three evaluation dimensions: (a) approach, (b) deployment, and (c) results.

- *Approach* refers to how the applicant addresses the requirements, that is, the methods used.

- *Deployment* refers to the extent to which the applicant's approach is applied to all requirements of the Award Criteria.

- *Results* refers to outcomes in achieving the purposes given in the Criteria. Factors used to evaluate results include current performance; performance relative to appropriate comparisons and benchmarks; rate, breadth and importance of performance improvements and demonstration of sustained improvement or high-level performance.

Of the Award's total value of 1,000 points, almost half are assigned to *business results*–customer satisfaction results, financial and market results, human resource results, supplier and partner results and company-specific results.

This focus on business results encompasses the customer's evaluation of the company's products and services, the company's overall financial and market performance and the results of key process and process improvement activities. All of these measures are aligned with the overall business strategy. Thus, the superior value of offerings as viewed by customers and the marketplace, and the superior company performance reflected in operational and financial indicators, are aligned.

An efficient way to reflect measured performance is to graphically project–on the same chart–past performance, current or actual performance with appropriate benchmarks and projected plan performance, as illustrated in Figure 17.

In performance analysis, the linkage of all measures should be considered–from the lowest process/operational level, to the intermediate/departmental level, to the business unit level. In devising the process performance

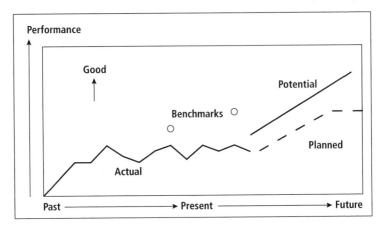

Figure 17. Performance reporting

scheme, appropriate in-process measures should be established as early in the process as is practicable.

To illustrate the general linkage of key service, quality and customer satisfaction performance measures, a matrix could be constructed of respective measures and indicators for customer satisfaction, operational/service, manufacturing/process/product and supplier measures (see Figure 18).

Several Baldrige Award winners have demonstrated effective use and linkage of key performance measurement. The following sections give some examples of how they have done so.

ADAC Laboratories. ADAC has initiated a customer-focused management system based on quality management principles as a way to change the company's culture. ADAC began with a primary core value—customers come

Supplier	Manufacturing/ Process/Product	Operational/Service	Key Customer Satisfaction Measures
Quality: • Reject rates • Rework Delivery: • On-time performance • Lead times	Defect levels (e.g., machining, molding, lining, scoring, printing, assembly) Scrap rates (e.g., machines, product, process) Other: • Spoilage rate • Video detection rate • Warranty costs • Reliability levels	Operational performance: • Down time • Lead time • Cycle time • Shortages • Idle time losses • Timeliness of releases • Changeover rate • Inventory accuracy • Shipping accuracy • Parts availability Service performance: • Technical/service delivery • Customer support "Hot line" response • Complaint follow-up • Emergency service response • Installation problems	Customer survey results ("Voice of the customer") Credits/returns Complaint rate Delivery performance a. Promised b. Requested

Figure 18.   Linkage of performance measures

first—and conducted a thorough, fact-based analysis of present and future customer requirements as part of the company's corporate planning process. Short- and long-term strategies were distilled into the "vital few" key business drivers that focus and align plans and continuous improvement efforts. These efforts now serve as the basis for *most important tasks* (MITs), or top priorities. At quarterly *measurement summits,* representatives from all departments review the collected data. Benchmarking is an integral element of ADAC's standardized problem-solving process and is used regularly by all continuous improvement teams to set performance goals and to gauge the effectiveness of management processes.

AT&T's Transmission Systems Business Unit. AT&T's Transmission Systems Business Unit (TSBU) uses eleven types of customer-related information—from report cards to various measures of the quality and responsiveness of customer-support services. Based on lessons learned from internal evaluations and benchmarking studies, TSBU's planning process is designed to create a clear cause-and-effect relationship among priorities, goals and subsequent improvement actions. Called *policy deployment,* the iterative process establishes links from AT&T's quality principles through TSBU's thirteen *detailed objectives* to the specific quality improvement projects carried out by more than 800 teams.

AT&T's Universal Card Services. AT&T's Universal Card Services (UCS) uses eight broad categories of *satisfiers,* including price and customer service, to define the company's quality focus. In turn, those prioritized determinants of how customers perceive the value of credit-card service are underpinned by 125 satisfiers, each one weighted to reflect its relative importance. A practical product of this increasing specificity is an exhaustive set of concrete performance measures linking internal operations to customer satisfaction. UCS's Customer Listening Post Team evaluates the effectiveness of procedures for gathering, responding to and evaluating customer comments and survey results. The team translates goals into key initiatives. At the top of the list are the ten most wanted quality improvements.

Dana Commercial Credit Corporation.   Dana Commercial Credit Corporation (DCC) provides leasing and financing services to a broad range of commercial customers. DCC has developed a collection of quality-linked *scoring processes* that assess how the company is doing in its pursuit of continuous improvement goals set for all key areas of the business. DCC's *SWOT analyses* (Strength or Weakness compared to the benchmark, as an Opportunity, or as a Threat to the business) compare company performance to benchmark measures in the key process areas.

Federal Express Corporation.   FedEx provides overnight, door-to-door delivery of documents and small package shipments. The company uses a quality improvement process focused on twelve *service quality indicators* (SQIs), all tied to customer expectations and articulated at all levels of its international business. To spur progress toward its ultimate target of 100-percent customer satisfaction, FedEx replaced its old measures of quality performance with a twelve-component index that comprehensively describes how its performance is viewed by customers. Each item in the SQI is weighted to reflect how significantly it affects overall customer satisfaction. Performance data are gathered with the company's advanced computer and tracking system, a handheld computer used for scanning a shipment's bar code every time a package changes hands between pick-up and delivery. Analysis of data contained in more than thirty major databases assists *quality action teams* (QATs) in locating the root causes of problems that surface in SQI reviews. The SQI measurements are linked directly to the corporate planning process, and executive bonuses rest upon how well the whole corporation meets performance improvement goals.

Motorola, Inc. Motorola, an integrated company that produces an array of products, established the corporate objective of total customer satisfaction with the company's quality goal, simply stated: "Zero defects in everything we do." To accomplish its goal, Motorola launched the now universally popularized Six Sigma Quality initiative.

Business Strategies

In order to achieve world-class levels of customer satisfaction, the organization must first recognize where it is on the spectrum of evolving business strategies. For customer focus to become a reality, the traditional business management styles must move toward the desired state outlined in Figure 19.

The necessity for cultural change was further exemplified by Ames Rubber Corporation (see Figure 20).

A service and quality improvement mentality can be institutionalized only within a climate conducive to change. Transition to such an *improvement culture* entails the following general stages:

1. Quality awareness: Commitment

2. Goals and objectives: Plan

3. Education and training: Transformation

4.   Quality improvement process: Implementation

5.   Information and results: Measurement

6.   Self-sufficiency: Excellence

	Traditional Style	Desired State
Application	Finished product	Process management
Responsibility	Quality department	Entire workforce/all employees
System	Inspection/detection	Prevention-based
Performance standard	Within specification	Continuous improvement
Priority	Budget and cost	Quality and service
Attention	Reaction to problems	Constancy of purpose
Problem solving	"Band-aid" approach	Root cause elimination
Culprits	Workers/employees	Management/system
Management styles	Managers were controlling	Identify expectation through shared goals and values
	People did what they were told	Focus on improvement not blame
	Lack of trust	Respect for the individual
	Large functional staff	Peel away layers of management
	Slow decision-making	Empowerment/authority to make decisions
	No accountability for business results	Measure based on both customer and shareholder performance

Figure 19.   *Evolving business strategies*

	From This	To This
Objectives	Short-term, undefined performance objectives and standards with frequent changes.	Long- and short-term objectives clearly stated and executed in a timely balanced manner.
Mangement Style	An authoritative mangement style with lack of trust and minimum involvement in risk taking and decision making.	A predominantly participative and open management style which encourages balanced risk taking and enables problems to be shared and solved cooperatively.
Teamwork	Internally competitive and narrow direction with low mutual esteem (win/lose style).	A team-oriented total company direction based on mutual respect and support (win/win style).
Customers	An environment in which there is an incomplete or ambiguous understanding of customer requirements.	An environment within which a systematic approach is used to understand and satisfy both internal and external customer requirements.
Peformance	An environment in which constant rework of tasks is acceptable as the norm.	An environment where task requirements are well defined and the expectation is that work is done right the first time. Constant striving for excellence and work improvement is a way of life.
Decision Making	An authoritative, unstructured, individualistic approach to problem solving and decision making.	A disciplined, predominantly participative approach to problem solving and decision making at all levels.

Figure 20. Cultural change

Adapted from Ames Rubber Corporation. Used with permission.

The overall impact of quality and service levels on the organization's financial performance can be demonstrated in many ways using respective company key financial indicators. For example, in dealing with *return on assets* (a common key financial indicator), the costs of nonconformances and the assets in place due to nonconformances, as well as potential lost opportunities, have a significant impact on revenue, costs and assets (see Figure 21).

To determine the impact of formal total quality management practices, the U.S. Congress asked the General

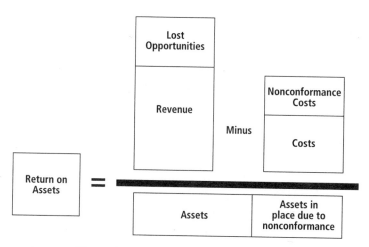

Figure 21. **Financial leverage of quality**

Accounting Office (GAO) to study the performance of selected companies in the United States. After reviewing companies that were among the highest-scoring applicants of the Malcolm Baldrige National Quality Award, the GAO concluded:

> *Companies that adopted quality management practices experienced an overall improvement in corporate performance. In nearly all cases, companies that used total quality management practices achieved better employee relations, higher productivity, greater customer satisfaction, increased market share, and improved profitability. Each of the companies studied developed its practices in a unique environment with its own opportunities and problems. . . However, none of these companies reaped those benefits immediately. Allowing sufficient time for results to be achieved was as important as initiating a quality management program.*

The report, titled *Management Practices: U.S. Companies Improve Performance Through Quality Efforts,* (GAO/NSIAD-91-190), can be obtained from the United States General Accounting Office, Washington, DC, 20548.

As a testimony to the power of the Malcolm Baldrige National Quality Award Criteria to improve and sustain business success, the stock performance of Baldrige Award winners was evaluated and reported. For four years in a row the "Baldrige Index" outperformed the Standard & Poor's (S&P) 500 stock index by almost three to one. Those companies that advanced to the final rounds of Baldrige judging, but did not receive the Award, outperformed the S&P index by more than two to one.

> *Through the Baldrige Award and the principles of quality management it embraces, countless businesses have found new and stronger life.* –William J. Clinton

CONCLUSION

Quality management is not just a strategy.
It must be a new style of working, even a new style
of thinking. A dedication to quality and excellence
is more than good business. It is a way of life.

George Bush

Customer-driven quality and service can provide the competitive advantage necessary in today's business environment. By focusing on customers, organizations can align their business strategies and goals with market expectations, thus enhancing customer satisfaction levels and improving operational performance.

In these few chapters, we have provided a *road map for success,* showing how companies can achieve competitive advantage through customer focus and process management (see Figure 22).

Using the Malcolm Baldrige National Quality Award framework for customer focus (Chapter 1), organizations can increase their customer and market knowledge, enhance their customer relationships and improve customer satisfaction.

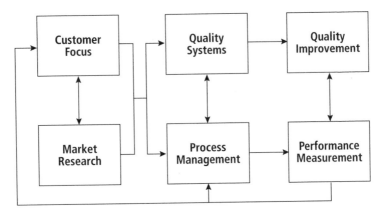

Figure 22.   Road map for success

By deploying applicable and effective quality system standards and procedures, organizations can achieve consistent process performance (Chapter 2).

Through appropriately designed and well-executed market research techniques (Chapter 3), organizations can analyze and use findings to drive companywide improvement actions, further strengthening internal performance and raising customer satisfaction levels.

Process management techniques (Chapter 4) are essential, beginning with quality awareness and effective quality system standards augmented by process analysis and meaningful quality planning.

The quality improvement process (Chapter 5), along with appropriate problem-solving and improvement tools, can help establish a climate conducive to change.

Proper alignment and consistency of key processes, performance measurement information and action plans are essential to achieving companywide business goals. When linked to key business drivers, service and quality performance measures (Chapter 6) can then serve as predictors of customer satisfaction and lead to further business success.

Appendix

ANSI/ISO/ASQ Standards
(Partial List)

Contractual quality standards:

- Q9001-1994: Quality Systems–Model for Quality Assurance in Design, Development, Production, Installation and Servicing

- Q9002-1994: Quality Systems–Model for Quality Assurance in Production, Installation and Servicing

- Q9003-1994: Quality Systems–Model for Quality Assurance in Final Inspection and Test

Selection, use and implementation guidelines:

- Q9000-1-1994: Quality Management and Quality Assurance Standards–Guidelines for Selection and Use

- Q9000-2-1993: Quality Management and Quality Assurance Standards–Generic Guidelines for the Application of ANSI/ISO/ASQ Q9001, 9002 and 9003

- Q9000-3-1991: Quality Management and Quality Assurance Standards–Guidelines for the Application of ANSI/ISO/ASQ 9001 to the Development, Supply and Maintenance of Software

- Q9004-1-1994: Quality Management and Quality System Elements–Guidelines

- Q9004-2-1991:Quality Management and Quality System Elements–Guidelines for Service

- Q9004-3-1993: Quality Management and Quality System Elements–Guidelines for Processed Materials

- Q9004-4-1993: Quality Management and Quality System Elements–Guidelines for Quality Improvement

- Q10006-1997: Quality Management–Guidelines for Quality in Project Management

- Q10007-1997: Quality Management–Guidelines for Configuration Management

- Q10011-1994: Guidelines for Auditing Quality Systems

- Q10012-1-1992: Quality Assurance Requirements for Measuring Equipment–Part 1: Metrological Confirmation System for Measuring Equipment

- Q10013-1995: Guidelines for Quality Manuals

- Q10014-1997: Guidelines for Managing the Economics of Quality

Standards may be obtained from the American Society for Quality, 611 East Wisconsin Avenue, P.O. Box 3005, Milwaukee, Wisconsin 53201.

PERMISSIONS
ACKNOWLEDGEMENTS

Grateful acknowledgement is made to the following for permission to adapt previously published material:

ADAC Laboratories

Aluminum Company of America

American Society for Quality (ASQ) Quality Press

AT&T

Ames Rubber Corporation

Eastman Chemical Company

Ford Motor Company

GTE Directories Corporation

IBM Corporation

FURTHER READING

Camp, Robert C., *Benchmarking: The Search for Industry Best Practices that Lead to Superior Performance,* Milwaukee, WI: ASQ Quality Press, 1989.

Caplan, Frank, *The Quality System: A Source Book for Managers and Engineers,* Radnor, PA: Chilton Book Company, 1990.

Galloway, Dianne, *Mapping Work Processes,* Milwaukee, WI: ASQ Quality Press, 1994.

Grant, Eugene L., and Richard S. Leavenworth, *Statistical Quality Control,* New York, NY: McGraw-Hill Book Company, 1995

Imai, Masaaki, *KAIZEN: The Key to Japan's Competitive Success,* New York, NY: Random House, Inc., 1986.

Peterson, Robert A., *Marketing Research,* Plano, TX: Business Publications, Inc., 1988

Stamatis, D. H., *Failure Mode and Effect Analysis: FMEA from Theory to Execution,* Milwaukee, WI, ASQ Quality Press, 1995.

Wilson, Paul F., Larry D. Dell, and Gaylord F. Anderson, *Root Cause Analysis: A Tool for Total Quality Management,* Milwaukee, WI: ASQ Quality Press, 1993.

About the Author

Roger G. Langevin is a leading authority on quality management, business performance improvement and customer satisfaction enhancement. He is the founder and principal consultant of Argyle Associates, Inc., a management consulting firm whose clients have included over fifty Fortune 500 corporations and more than 100 medium-sized and smaller companies worldwide.

Mr. Langevin's diverse career has included positions at the leading edge of quality technology. He served as the quality assurance manager on the Apollo Applications Program with Grumman Aerospace Corporation and as a vice president with Chase Manhattan Bank, where he was responsible for quality control and customer service of bank operations.

He is an elected Fellow of the American Society for Quality (ASQ), a former member of ASQ's Board of Directors, and a Certified Quality Engineer, and has served on the Malcolm Baldrige National Quality Award Board of Directors for six years. Mr. Langevin holds a BME degree from The City College of New York and an MS(IE) degree from New York University.

Roger G. Langevin, Argyle Associates, Inc., One Robin Woods Lane, South Salem, NY 10590 U.S.A.